ESSENTIAL

INTERNET

GETTING CONNECTED

ABOUT THIS BOOK

Getting Connected is an easy-to-follow guide to connecting your PC to the Internet, and an introduction to all that the Net has to offer, including the World Wide Web and email.

THIS BOOK WILL HELP YOU GET connected with Windows 98, which contains all the software you need to connect you to the Internet and to find your virtual feet there. It will help you to choose the right modem and Internet Service Provider for your needs, and then help you make your first connection to the Net. It will also show you how to get started on the Web, how to send email, read newsgroups, and chat online with other Net users. You will soon be able to search for information on the Net, save Web pages that are of particular interest, download software to your own computer, and even access games to play. The final chapters of the book explain the basics of email, newsgroups, and chatting live over the Internet.

Within each chapter, you will find subsections that also deal with self-contained procedures. Each of these procedures builds on the knowledge that you will have accumulated by working through the previous chapters.

The chapters and the subsections use a methodical step-by-step approach. Almost

This book is designed for anyone who is taking their first steps into the exciting world of the Internet.

every step is accompanied by an illustration showing how your screen should look. The screen images either show the full screen or they focus on an important detail that you will see on your own screen. As you work through the steps, you will soon start to feel comfortable that you are learning and making progress.

The book contains several other features that make it easier to absorb the huge amount of information that is provided. Cross-references are shown within the text as left- or right-hand page icons: and . The page number within the icon and the reference are shown at the foot of the page.

As well as the step-by-step sections, there are boxes that explain the meaning of unfamiliar terms and abbreviations, and give additional information to take your knowledge beyond that provided on the rest of the page. Finally, at the back, you will find a glossary explaining new terms and a comprehensive index.

For further information on using the Internet, see *Browsing The Web* and *Em@il* in this *DK Essential Computers* series.

ESSENTIAL **DK** COMPUTERS

INTERNET

GETTING CONNECTED

BRIAN COOPER

A Dorling Kindersley Book

Dorling Kindersley
LONDON, NEW YORK, DELHI, SYDNEY,
PARIS, MUNICH, JOHANNESBURG

Produced for Dorling Kindersley Limited by
Design Revolution, Queens Park Villa,
30 West Drive, Brighton, East Sussex BN2 2GE

EDITORIAL DIRECTOR Ian Whitelaw
SENIOR DESIGNER Andy Ashdown
PROJECT EDITOR John Watson
DESIGNER Andrew Easton

MANAGING EDITOR Sharon Lucas
SENIOR MANAGING ART EDITOR Derek Coombes
DTP DESIGNER Sonia Charbonnier
PRODUCTION CONTROLLER Wendy Penn

Published in Great Britain in 2000 by
Dorling Kindersley Limited,
9 Henrietta Street, London WC2E 8PS

2 4 6 8 10 9 7 5 3

A CIP catalog record for this book is available from the British Library.

ISBN 0-7513-0994-X

Color reproduced by First Impressions, London
Printed in Italy by Graphicom

For our complete
catalog visit
www.dk.com

CONTENTS

THE INTERNET

The Internet is a network of millions of computers, offering information, communication, and a wealth of online activities. This chapter describes what it is and how it works.

WHAT CAN YOU DO ON THE INTERNET?

As you read this sentence, millions of people are using the Internet. They may be browsing documents on the World Wide Web, exchanging messages by email, chatting "live" in 3D virtual worlds, downloading the latest software, or playing 3D interactive games against players from all over the world.

Your ISP
The Internet Service Provider acts as the gateway through which the data passes to and from your computer.

Your computer
You access the Internet from your PC connected by a modem to an ISP.

Telephone line

Modem
A modem turns digital data into an analog signal to send over the telephone lines to your ISP, and converts received signals into a digital form.

Servers
Your data passes through a series of servers to reach its final destination.

"Backbones"
High speed communication links.

Local Access
Any user, anywhere in the world, can access the Internet for the cost of a local phone call (to her/his ISP).

In some fortunate areas of the world, there are no call charges at all!

WHAT IS THE INTERNET?

The Internet, in physical terms, is a vast global network made up from many thousands of computer networks and individual computers. The Internet "works" because these computers and computer networks can all speak the same language, called TCP/IP (which stands for Transmission Control Protocol/Internet Protocol).

For most people, the Internet is the same thing as the World Wide Web and all the Web addresses that appear everywhere these days – on product packaging, at the end of TV shows, and on junk mail. But there is more to the Internet than the Web.

There are vast networks of computers devoted to newsgroups, bulletin boards and discussion groups ⌐, and thousands of servers across the world are devoted to online "chat" areas ⌐.

But the Web is the part of the Internet that has seen a rapid explosion in popularity and ease-of-use.

WHAT'S ON THE INTERNET?

The Internet offers information on just about every topic you care to think of. Whether your interests include current affairs, astrophysics, golf, or Antarctic flora and fauna, there is almost certain to be a website devoted to that topic somewhere.

The Net has always been the home of academic information, but it has increasingly become an information base for public sector bodies, government departments, individuals, and, most recently, commercial organizations.

Online games
Pit your wits against opponents all round the world with online games.

Email
Communicate with people around the globe for just the price of a local call.

Shopping
Online shopping is becoming very big business on the Web.

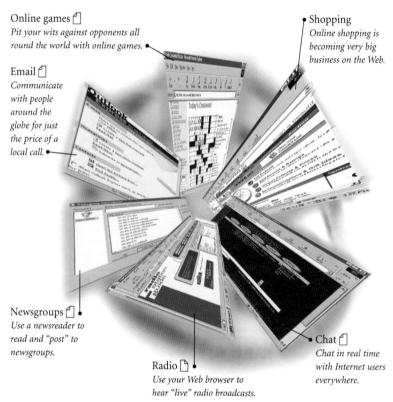

Newsgroups
Use a newsreader to read and "post" to newsgroups.

Radio
Use your Web browser to hear "live" radio broadcasts.

Chat
Chat in real time with Internet users everywhere.

REQUIREMENTS

If you have Windows 98 installed on your computer, you will already have the software required to connect to the Internet. But you also need a modem and an account with an Internet Service Provider to make a connection.

MODEM

If you don't have a modem ⌐, you will need to buy and install one. If your PC is running Windows 98, it can handle what the Internet has to offer, although as video, audio, and real-time broadcasts become more widespread, you'll inevitably begin to think about the need to upgrade your modem or computer hardware.

SERVICE PROVIDER

With a PC and modem you need one more element to get connected. That's where your Internet Service Provider (ISP) comes in ⌐. There are numerous ISPs, and many offer free connection and unlimited time online. Some ISPs are obviously more reliable than others, so many users prefer to pay for a proven service.

Your modem connects you to an ISP's systems room

HARDWARE REQUIREMENTS

In order to connect to the Internet you will need: a computer, a modem and connecting cable, and an active telephone line.

⌐12 **Modems**

⌐19 **Choosing a Service Provider**

SOFTWARE AND HARDWARE

Microsoft® Internet Explorer is one of the most popular Web-browsing programs and offers all the facilities that you need to browse the Web and become part of the online community.

WHAT CAN EXPLORER DO?

Internet Explorer comes as a standard part of Windows 98 software and is usually pre-installed on most new computers. Internet Explorer is more than just a Web-browsing program: it is a suite of programs enabling most Internet-related activities, from browsing the Web and composing and sending email, to taking the plunge and publishing your own Web pages. Outlook Express is the name of the email program and newsreader that comes with Internet Explorer, and FrontPage® is Microsoft's Web-publishing program. Both these programs are the subject of their own books in this series, but a brief description of all three of these programs will help to give you an idea of what each of them can do and how they are interrelated.

WHAT IS EXPLORER?

Internet Explorer is the Web-browsing program that enables you to connect to Websites and view them ⌐, surf the Web using hypertext links, and download files and programs from the Internet to your own computer ⌐. By default, its email features operate through Outlook Express.

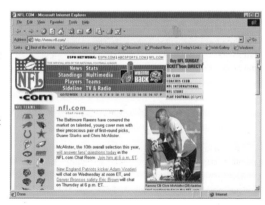

OUTLOOK EXPRESS

Outlook Express is an email program that you can use to send and receive email 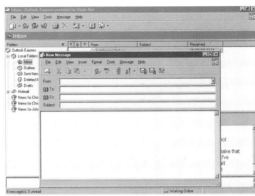, manage your own online address book 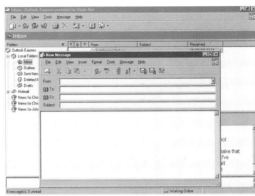, and exchange files and information with others over the Internet. It also contains a fully featured newsreader for reading and posting messages to Internet newsgroups.

FRONTPAGE

Eventually, the time may come when you want to create your own Web pages. FrontPage helps you to do just that. It provides a Web-page editor that enables you to build Web pages with only a minimal understanding of HyperText Markup Language (HTML), the language in which Web pages are constructed.

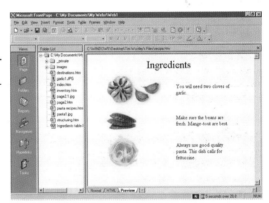

INSTALLING OTHER COMPONENTS

If Outlook Express or FrontPage are not on your computer, you can install them from your Windows or Internet Explorer CD-ROM. If you cannot locate your disks, another option open to you is to download a new version of Internet Explorer from the Microsoft Website and reinstall the entire program on your computer, making sure that you elect to install these additional programs during the installation process. Click the **Microsoft** button on the **Links** bar to go to Microsoft's Website.

| 56 | How To Send a Message |
| 58 | Setting Up the Address Book |

MODEMS

Without a modem in your computer or connected externally, your connection to the Internet remains purely theoretical! The next few pages are devoted to one of the most commonly used types of modem: the 56K V90-compliant external modem. This is capable of receiving data at 56,000 bits per second.

WHAT IS A MODEM?

A modem is a piece of equipment that connects your PC to the Internet via the telephone lines. In very simple terms, a modem converts digital (binary) signals from your computer into analog (sound) signals that can be sent along telephone lines. At the same time, it converts incoming analog signals into binary signals (basically, strings of 1s and 0s) that your computer can understand.

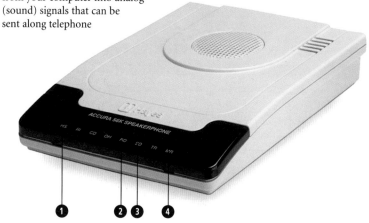

MODEM FRONT PANEL

❶ HS – High Speed
This light illuminates if the modem is operating at speeds in excess of 4,800bps.

❷ RD – Receiving Data
This light indicates whether or not your modem is "idle."

❸ SD – Sending Data
This light is active when you are sending data.

❹ MR – Modem Ready
This light shows that the modem is switched on and ready for use.

WHAT IS ISDN?

Integrated Service Digital Network lines can send digital rather than analog information over existing telephone lines at very high speeds, achieving rates of between 64,000 bps and 300,000 bps. It is virtually error-free and can be used to transmit voice. To use ISDN, however, you will need to use special hardware, software, and a different telephone connection and ISP account than those featured in this book. Some service providers charge higher rates for ISDN connections but many do not.

AN EXTERNAL MODEM

The modem in these photographs is a Hayes Accura 56K Speakerphone. This is a good example of an external modem as it has many features, including answering machine, fax, and speakerphone. Obviously there are many other modems available, and some of these may have differing features. The annotation on this example therefore only explains the major features.

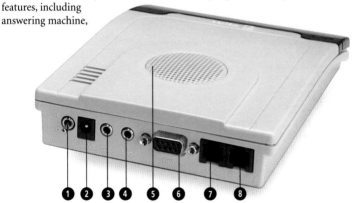

MODEM BACK PANEL

❶ On/Off Switch
❷ Connector
Power supply.
❸ Speaker Connection
❹ Microphone Connection

❺ Speaker
❻ Serial Port (DTE Interface)
For connecting your computer to the modem.

❼ Line
Plug one end of your telephone cable in here.
❽ Phone
To use a telephone on the same line as the modem.

Software for External Modems

When you buy an external modem, it will usually come with its own software on a CD or floppy disk set. Follow the instructions in the manual carefully and you should have few problems installing the software on your computer. The example below shows the software that comes with the Hayes Accura 56K Speakerphone, as shown on the previous pages. Your software may look different, but this screen shows features common to similar modems.

Telephone facility
Shows last call and has its own telephone book, where you can enter your favorite numbers. You can "dial" numbers straight from your keyboard.

Answering machine/Voicemail
Enables easy set-up of voicemail and answering machine messages. Play, forward, and rewind messages from this panel.

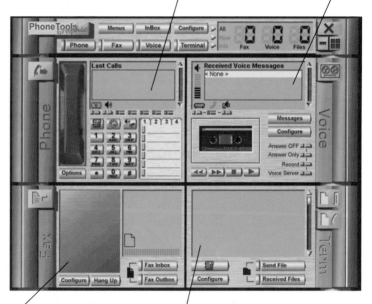

Fax
From this panel you can set up the software to fax a document from any Windows application.

Terminal emulation
Connect to various online services to retrieve information, upload and download files, etc.

CHOOSING A MODEM

The most important thing to consider when buying a modem is speed. You want the fastest modem you can afford. The fastest modem currently available is a 56K modem. This means that it is capable of receiving data at 56 Kilobytes per second (although it is only capable of sending data at a maximum of 33.6 Kbps).

WHAT NEXT?

After finding the fastest, most reliable, most economical modem, you need to choose between an internal and external model. If your PC came with an internal modem installed, this won't really concern you – yet. But if modems continue to increase in speed (and drop in price) you may soon find that you want to replace your existing modem.

External modems are very easy to install. There are two stages to installation: first, physical installation (which basically involves plugging things in), and secondly software configuration (which is usually "automatic" with Windows 98).

Installing or replacing an internal modem isn't too difficult either, but if you don't feel happy about taking off the case of your computer and installing a card on the PC's motherboard (remembering to wear an anti-static wrist strap) then you have two choices: either get your hardware dealer to install it for you, or buy an external modem.

One of the major advantages of an external modem is that the lights on the casing indicate the status of your connection, making it easier to know when to restart your Internet connection, simply by switching off your modem. With an internal modem, if there is a problem with your Internet connection, you may need to restart your computer.

Internal modem
Installing a card on the mother-board of a PC can seem an intimidating task, but is actually fairly straightforward.

INSTALLING AN EXTERNAL MODEM

Connecting an external modem is usually a straightforward task. It is important to read the manufacturer's instructions in case there are any special requirements, but most installations follow the procedure described here.

1 PREPARING TO INSTALL
• Switch off your PC and unplug from the main power supply.

2 CONNECTING POWER SUPPLY
• Connect your modem to the power supply using the cable and/or power adapter provided.

3 CONNECTING SERIAL CABLE
• Attach one end of the serial cable to the modem, and the other end to a vacant serial cable on your PC. This will usually be the COM 1 port, but if your mouse is already installed there, use the COM 2 port.

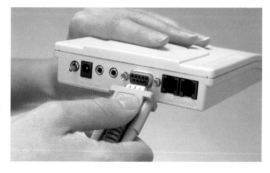

4 TELEPHONE LINE

● Connect the modem's telephone cable between the appropriate socket on the back of the modem and the telephone socket. Switch on the modem. One or more of the indicator lights will light up.

CONFIGURING YOUR MODEM

If you are installing a modem that is not accompanied with installation software, Windows 98 will usually detect its make and model automatically. It will then attempt to install all the drivers necessary to make your modem perform effectively. You may find, however, that Windows 98 needs help to locate the appropriate software for your modem. This is usually solved simply by following these steps:

1 MODEMS ICON

● Double-click the **Modems** icon; the **Install New Modem** dialog box will appear.

2 SELECTING MODEM

● Click on the check box next to **Don't detect my modem; I will select it from a list** to tick it, and then click **Next>**.

Checkbox

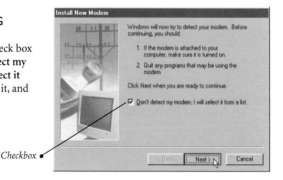

3 MANUFACTURER AND MODEL

● Click the appropriate entry under **Manufacturers** and **Models**, then click **Next>**. (If the manufacturer has supplied a disk, click **Have Disk…**, navigate to the appropriate location for the CD-ROM or floppy disk, and follow the on-screen instructions.)

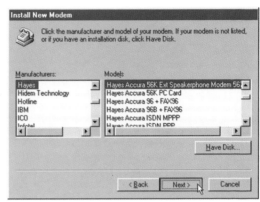

4 SELECTING A PORT

● Click **Communications Port (COM 1)** and then click **Next>**. (This may be **COM 2** if a mouse is already installed on COM 1.)

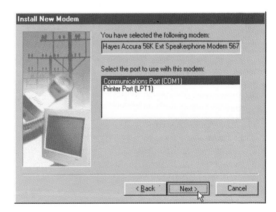

5 COMPLETING THE PROCESS

● Provide the necessary information in the location information dialog box and click **Finish**. Your modem is now ready to use.

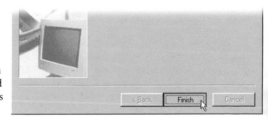

CHOOSING A SERVICE PROVIDER

An Internet Service Provider (ISP) provides your gateway to the Internet – usually via an ordinary telephone line.

Your ISP will provide you with a local telephone number (a point of presence) which gives you access to its servers.

DIAL-UP ACCESS

This access to servers is known as "dial-up access." If an ISP doesn't provide you with a dial-up connection charged at local rates (or free), you're not interested! An ISP provides you with a number of Internet services: access to the Web ⌐, a unique email address (perhaps several) ⌐, and access to thousands of newsgroups ⌐. Most ISPs also give you space on their servers to post your own Web pages. You may be provided with free software to do all or some of these things.

These are now standard services and should be provided by your ISP.

HOW DO I CHOOSE THE RIGHT ONE?

Choosing the right ISP was much simpler a few years back. If you lived outside urban areas, it was usually a case of finding one that offered Internet access at local call

THE INTERNET-READY PC

Most new PCs are advertised as "Internet-ready." This means that they contain an internal modem, and a ready-to-go Internet account, in which case your ISP is already chosen for you.

rates – if you were lucky! Nowadays, service providers (many offering national coverage) are falling over each other to win your custom, so it's never been a better time to get connected.

The old established ISPs have improved, and newer start-ups are offering excellent deals. A wave of "free" ISPs has also arrived – some are freer than others ⌐.

Meanwhile, the big online service providers (AOL, Prodigy, CompuServe and MSN) have changed their approach to meet the challenge.

Weigh up the pros and cons…
Choosing an Internet Service Provider needn't be a chore, but should be looked into carefully so you find one that has all the facilities you need.

32 Onto The Web

27 Setting Up an Email Account

62 Newsgroups

21 Questions to ask an ISP

HOW DOES AN ISP WORK?

Although it seems you are connected directly to the Internet when you are browsing through Web pages, all the data you send and receive is actually passing down a lot of cable and through many other computers (servers) before it reaches your screen. All this technical stuff is handled in the background by your ISP.

WHEN YOU ARE CONNECTED

Each time you dial up to the Internet, your data is first received and processed by your ISP. If you are requesting data from, or sending data to, the Internet, your ISP routes the information via one of its very fast connections to the Internet.

If you are requesting or sending email, data is sent to the ISP's mail servers – one for incoming and one for outgoing mail 🗋.

To improve speed of access to the Web, many ISPs provide a proxy server. This is a computer that stores all the current copies of Web pages that have been requested by its customers so that, when another customer requests one, it can return the information more quickly.

Regular traveler?

If you want to be able to dial your ISP at local rates from anywhere in the country, choose one that offers national coverage. Some ISPs, and most online services, have many international points of presence 🗋.

ISP OR ONLINE SERVICE?

In the past, your choice of service provider split evenly between basic ISPs (offering email, unlimited access to the Internet, and newsgroups), and online services that offered large networks of well organized, authoritative information, members-only email and chat areas, and access to the Web.

In recent years, the difference between the two has become less distinct. Many ISPs now offer well-organized gateways to the Internet. Apart from content, the main difference between online services and ISPs is cost. Online services generally charge a basic monthly rate which is much lower than many ISPs offer, but is for a fixed number of hours per month. Most ISPs charge a fixed monthly rate for unlimited access.

- Apparel
- Art & Collectibles
- Auctions & Outlets
- Books, Music & Video
- Computing
- Consumer Electronics
- Dept. Stores
- Flowers & Gifts
- Food & Wine
- Health & Beauty
- Home & Garden
- Home Office
- Jewelry & Accessories
- Kids, Toys & Babies
- Pets
- Sports & Outdoors
- Travel & Auto

Channels available
These options are offered by AOL.

QUESTIONS TO ASK AN ISP

Do you charge a registration or sign-up fee?

What do you charge per month?

Are there any additional charges; e.g. for time online, technical support, software, anything else?

Can I dial up using a number charged at local rate?
(Some ISPs offer free calls as part of the package, but these are currently rare.)

Do you offer a free trial?

How many email addresses do you offer?
(More than one email address is useful if several family members are to share the email account.)

Do you offer POP3 mail?
(This is essential if you want to receive mail on a remote computer.)

Which newsgroups will I be able to access?
(Some ISPs offer a limited number of newsgroups, blocking some of those containing adult content.)

What software do you provide?

What customer support/technical support do you offer?

It may be handy to photocopy this page and use it to make notes when you are telephoning different ISPs.

CONNECTING

Once you have chosen your Internet Service Provider, and have
either the sign-up software on a CD or all the ISP's details, you
are ready to make your first connection to the Internet.

USING AN ISP'S SOFTWARE TO CONNECT

If your ISP has provided you with sign-up
software, making a connection should be
simply a matter of inserting the ISP's CD
and following the on-screen instructions.

It is in the interests of ISPs (especially
those offering you a free trial period) to
make the signing-up procedure as simple,
quick, and error-free as possible.

SUPPLYING DETAILS

When you insert the ISP's
CD, you will be asked to
make a series of choices
regarding the installation
of software, and to supply
some personal details (e.g.
your name, age, address,
and probably information
about hobbies and
interests). Unless you are
signing up with a "free" ISP
you will also probably be
asked to supply payment
(usually credit card) details.

EXPIRATION DATES

Watch the expiration date
of free trials! If you gave
payment details when you
signed up for a free trial, it
is usually up to you to
cancel the payment if you
decide not to continue
with the service. Otherwise
the monthly amount will
be debited from your
account once the free trial
is over.

USING MORE THAN ONE ISP

On the following pages, we describe how to set up a connection to an ISP using the "dial-up networking" software that is supplied with Windows 98.

This method is particularly recommended if you decide to use (or try out) more than one ISP, because it provides a simple and neat solution.

WHY NEAT?

Prodigy Internet

If you install more than one account you may find that the most recent installation has customized your browser and changed your default email settings. This might be just a cosmetic change, but sometimes the changes affect the default settings for your Internet software. The new ISP may set itself up as the connection that launches whenever you open Internet Explorer or Outlook Express and all your email will carry the address connected with that ISP. These settings can be changed

Connection to EZ-ISP

Connection to Bigstores.net

back to your preferred settings, but it can be irritating.

The advantage of using the "dial-up networking" method, which is described on the following pages, is that each connection is kept separate from any other. When you create a dial-up networking "session," it contains all the information relating to a single ISP. Then, whenever you double-click the icon, you are connected to that ISP, leaving your Web browser and mail settings unaffected.

CompuServe

WHY USE MORE THAN ONE ISP?

PROS

If you use several ISPs, you reduce the chances of being unable to connect to the Net at any time, or send or receive your email. If one ISP's servers are out of action for any reason, you simply dial-up to another ISP and connect to the Net by this alternative route. If you have access to any genuinely free ISPs it makes sense to have at least one alternative route to the Net.

CONS

If you have too many Internet accounts and email addresses, it can become time-consuming to collect your mail. Also, your friends will give up mailing you altogether if you keep sending them new email addresses. One solution to this is to use one mail account only. You can set up Outlook Express to retrieve mail from any POP3 server, regardless of the ISP with which you are connected.

CONNECTING MANUALLY TO YOUR ISP

Before you begin the next steps, it is important to make sure that you have all the necessary information at hand (see box below). Your ISP should supply you with all of these settings.

Finally, with this information at your fingertips, and your modem switched on and connected to an active telephone socket, you are ready to make your first connection to the Internet. And this next part is really very easy.

Note that the following instructions only apply to the first account that you set up with an ISP. Instructions are given later in the book on how you should go about adding any subsequent accounts.

CONNECTION SETTINGS YOU WILL NEED

• **Your user name and password**
These may be specified by your ISP, or your ISP may have asked you to choose them yourself over the telephone. The important thing is that the user name and password are those that you have agreed with your ISP.

• **Your ISP's phone number**
This is the number you will be dialing to connect to the Internet.

• **A second user name and password**
Some ISPs require a second user name to allow you to access your email. Most ISPs require you to have a password different from your main password

specifically to allow you to access your incoming email.

• **The ISP's mail server addresses**
There will usually be two of these, one for incoming mail and one for outgoing mail. These addresses will look something like this:
   smtp.cdotn.com *(outgoing)*
   pop3.cdotn.com *(incoming)*

• **The address of your ISP's news server**
This will be something like this:
   news.cdotn.com.

• **Any additional settings**
These may be required by the ISP and are likely to relate to DNS settings and a proxy server. It doesn't matter for now what these settings do, but it is important that you have a note of them right at the start.

1 START CONNECTING

● Double-lick the **Connect to the Internet** icon on your desktop.

2 SET UP MANUALLY

● Check the radio button next to **I want to set up my Internet connection manually...** and click **Next>**.

Click the radio button ●

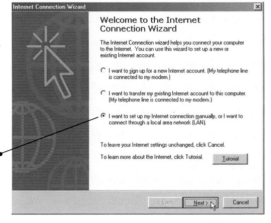

Internet Connection Wizard

Welcome to the Internet Connection Wizard

The Internet Connection wizard helps you connect your computer to the Internet. You can use this wizard to set up a new or existing Internet account.

○ I want to sign up for a new Internet account. (My telephone line is connected to my modem.)

○ I want to transfer my existing Internet account to this computer. (My telephone line is connected to my modem.)

⦿ I want to set up my Internet connection manually, or I want to connect through a local area network (LAN).

To leave your Internet settings unchanged, click Cancel.

To learn more about the Internet, click Tutorial. [Tutorial]

< Back   Next >   Cancel

3 USING THE MODEM

● In the next dialog box, check the radio button next to **I connect through a phone line and a modem** and then click **Next>**.

Click the radio button ●

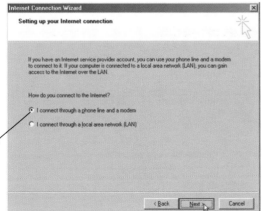

Internet Connection Wizard

Setting up your Internet connection

If you have an Internet service provider account, you can use your phone line and a modem to connect to it. If your computer is connected to a local area network (LAN), you can gain access to the Internet over the LAN.

How do you connect to the Internet?

⦿ I connect through a phone line and a modem

○ I connect through a local area network (LAN)

< Back   Next >   Cancel

4 TELEPHONE NUMBER

• Type your ISP's telephone number (the one that you have been given for your Internet connection) and click **Next>**. Ignore the **Advanced...** button for now. If necessary, you can type additional settings later ⌐.

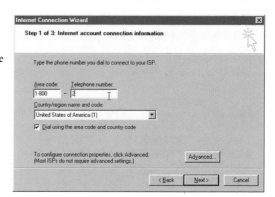

5 USER NAME

• Type your User name and password, and click **Next>**.

Enter name ●

6 IDENTIFY CONNECTION

• Type a name, which can be any text string, to identify the connection. The name is a convenient way to identify the connection and does not affect your dialing-in to your ISP. It is safer just to call this connection the name of your ISP, particularly if you collect a number of accounts. When you have done this, click **Next>**.

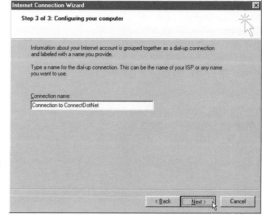

⌐30 Advanced Connection Settings

SETTING UP AN EMAIL ACCOUNT

The next few steps relate to setting up your email account. If, for any reason, you don't have all of your email settings at hand (perhaps, for example, you still need to check your POP3 server's address with your ISP) you will be prompted for the same details the first time you try to launch Outlook Express.

1 SETTING UP THE ACCOUNT
● In the next dialog box, click the **Yes** button in answer to **Do you want to set up an Internet account now?** Then click **Next>**.

Click Yes ●

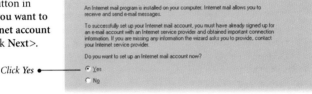

2 ENTERING THE NAME
● Type a name in the display box that will appear in the **From** part of your email messages – the name that recipients of your messages will see.

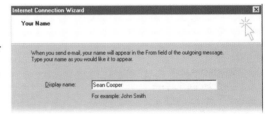

3 ENTERING THE ADDRESS
● Type your email address, as agreed with your ISP.

4 ADDING SERVER ADDRESSES

● Type the address for the **Incoming mail (POP3, IMAP or HTTP)** and **Outgoing mail (SMTP) servers,** as supplied by your ISP.

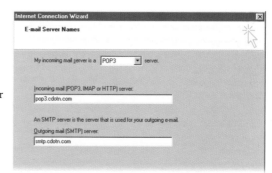

5 ACCOUNT NAME AND PASSWORD

● Type the **Account name** and **Password** required to access your incoming email ⌐⌐. You may choose to click on the **Remember password** box too ⌐.

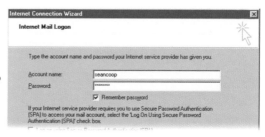

6 MAKING THE CONNECTION

● Check the box **To connect to the Internet immediately…** and then click on **Finish** to make a connection to your ISP.

Check here ●

Completing the Internet Connection Wizard

You have successfully completed the Internet Connection wizard.
Your computer is now configured to connect to your Internet account.

After you close this wizard, you can connect to the Internet at any time by double-clicking the Internet Explorer icon on your desktop.

☑ To connect to the Internet immediately, select this box and then click Finish.

To close the wizard, click Finish

< Back   Finish   Cancel

| 24 | Connection settings you will need |

| 29 | Password Security |

7 CONNECTING TO THE WEB

● The **Dial-up Connection** box appears. Type your password if necessary and click **Connect**. You should now be connected to the Internet. Double-click the **Internet Explorer** icon on your desktop and watch the Web appear on your computer!

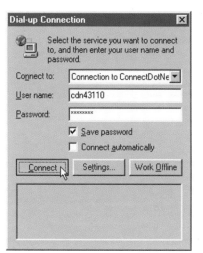

PASSWORDS

It is essential that you keep a note of your passwords somewhere private – they may seem memorable at the time, but may not be a year later. (Websites frequently ask you to assign yourself a user name and password to access their content.)

PASSWORD SECURITY

How you use the **Remember password** checkbox, when it appears, is entirely a matter of choice. If you are the only user of your PC then it is a useful feature. It means you don't have to type your password every time you connect to the Internet, or collect your email.

If you share your computer with other users, however, you may want to keep certain things password-protected. For example, you may prefer to restrict the access that any children in the household have to certain areas of the Internet or to your personal mailbox.

ADVANCED CONNECTION SETTINGS

In many cases you will not need to use any "advanced" settings. They may not be required by your ISP, or may have been set up automatically. The most likely setting you will need to make is to specify that your Web browser uses your ISP's proxy server ☐. This will speed up access to Web pages. To do this, follow these steps:

1 INTERNET OPTIONS
● In the Windows 98 **Start** menu choose **Settings** and then **Control Panel**. Now double-click the **Internet Options** icon and click the **Connections** tab.

Internet Options

2 SETTING THE ISP CONNECTION
● On the **Connections** page of the **Internet Properties** dialog box, click the name that identifies the connection to your ISP and click **Settings**.

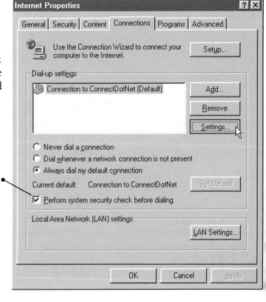

Select for security check ●
(allows you to turn off sharing – if you have shared folders on your computer – before connecting to the Net)

Internet Properties ? ✕

General | Security | Content | Connections | Programs | Advanced

Use the Connection Wizard to connect your computer to the Internet.   Setup...

Dial-up settings

Connection to ConnectDotNet (Default)   Add...

   Remove

   Settings...

○ Never dial a connection
○ Dial whenever a network connection is not present
◉ Always dial my default connection

Current default: Connection to ConnectDotNet   Set Default

☑ Perform system security check before dialing

Local Area Network (LAN) settings

   LAN Settings...

OK | Cancel | Apply

20 **When you are connected**

3 USING A PROXY SERVER

● Check the **Use a proxy server** box and in the boxes provided type the **Address** and **Port** number (usually 8080) supplied by your ISP. Then click **OK** to return to the **Internet Properties** dialog box, and click **OK** again.

● The settings you type on the next screen will only affect the dial-up networking session you have highlighted here. (Clearly, this is only relevant if you have accounts with more than one ISP.)

Connection to ConnectDotNet Settings ? X

Automatic configuration

Automatic configuration may override manual settings. To ensure the use of manual settings, disable automatic configuration.

☐ Automatically detect settings

☐ Use automatic configuration script

Address [ ]

Proxy server

☑ Use a proxy server

Address: [ ] Port: [ ] Advanced...

☐ Bypass proxy server for local addresses

Dial-up settings

User name: cdn43110 Properties

Password: ✕✕✕✕✕✕✕✕ Advanced

Domain: (optional) [ ]

☐ Do not allow Internet programs to use this connection

OK Cancel

CONGRATULATIONS!

Well, that's all the technical stuff over with. Now you are connected, nothing can hold you back – except maybe time and an awareness of telephone charges (if you're unfortunate enough to have to pay them). So get on the Web, follow those links, and marvel at the sheer scale of the Internet! Once the initial surfing frenzy has worn off, you will soon realize how important it is to organize your time online effectively. How do you do that? Well, knowing exactly what your Internet software can do is a useful starting point. Then knowing how to find exactly what you want (and always making a note of the address where you found it) is another great time-saver.

Later in this book you will learn how to start using Internet Explorer and Outlook Express . You will also get an idea of where you can visit to put your new knowledge to immediate effect !

ONTO THE WEB

Perhaps the best known aspect of the Internet is the World Wide Web. To find your way around it and locate Websites, you need to use a Web browser and search engines.

WHAT IS A WEB BROWSER?

A Web browser is a piece of software installed on your PC that enables you to look at (or "browse") Websites. The most popular Web browsers are Netscape Navigator and Microsoft Internet Explorer. You can have both of them installed on your PC, and which one you use is a matter of personal preference.

WHICH BROWSER?
The examples shown in this book use Microsoft Internet Explorer, but the pages should look almost the same using Netscape Navigator. New versions of these browsers are released from time to time, adding new features. It is best to use the most recent release of either browser, providing your PC has sufficient memory and processing power to support it.

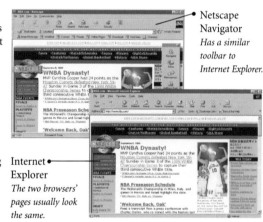

Netscape
Navigator
Has a similar toolbar to Internet Explorer.

Internet •
Explorer
The two browsers' pages usually look the same.

MORE ABOUT BROWSERS

Two browsers may make the same Website look slightly different because they have interpreted the language in which the Web pages are written (Hypertext Markup Language or HTML) in a different way.

WHAT'S ON THE WEB?

The World Wide Web is perhaps the best known aspect of the Internet. Around the world, computers called servers store pages on Websites created by organizations, individuals, and commercial companies, and any computer user who is connected to the Internet can access these Websites. Some sites exist purely to provide free information, or promote charitable causes, while others offer services or goods for sale, or charge the user to view material, or to play computer games online.

Nonprofit organizations
Most major charities and non-profit organizations promote their work on the Web.

News
Broadcast corporations provide up-to-the-minute news of global events on the Web, often before it goes out over the airwaves.

Education
Many leading universities and independent bodies offer courses that can be taken over the Web.

Online games
You can pit your wits against opponents all around the world with online games.

Commercial organizations
You can buy almost anything over the Web, from books and clothes to your weekly groceries.

Research
Libraries, universities, public and commercial bodies, and individuals all publish information on the Web.

Government bodies
To email the President or contact your local council, you will almost certainly find the right address on a Website.

Hobbyists
Individuals create their own Websites on topics of interest, but amateur information is not always reliable.

WHAT'S ON A WEB PAGE?

In the early days of the Web, Web pages contained only text and very basic formatting, offering very little in the way of design. Today's Web pages are a world away from those of the early pioneers, with many sites aspiring to be multimedia extravaganzas. A Web page is likely to incorporate sophisticated graphics, video clips, sound sequences, interactive animations, and miniature software programs known as "applets," on the page.

Download files
Web pages can contain files that you transfer to your own computer to view or install.

Programs
While you are viewing a Web page, a program can run independently.

Graphics
A well-designed Website can be a showcase for the skills of the graphic designer.

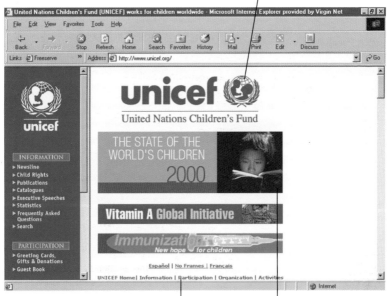

Text
Text within a page can be copied, pasted, and saved to your hard disk.

Hypertext links
Use hypertext links, or "hyperlinks," to go directly to other relevant sites.

Photographs
Images on a Web page can also act as hyperlinks.

Multimedia files
These can be sound, video, or interactive animations.

HOW A WEB PAGE WORKS

Web pages are built using a computer language called HyperText Markup Language (HTML). HTML comprises a set of tags that identify the elements on a Web page as being of a certain type – for example, text, image, or multimedia file. The HTML tags tell the Web browser where to find the files to build the page, how to display them, and the tags act as the glue that binds the files together.

Browser window
This is how the Web page appears in the browser window.

HTML tag
This line tells the browser that the file is a HyperText Markup document.

HTML code
This code tells the browser how to display a Web page. HTML instructions are known as "tags." View the code of a page by choosing "View Source" in your Web browser.

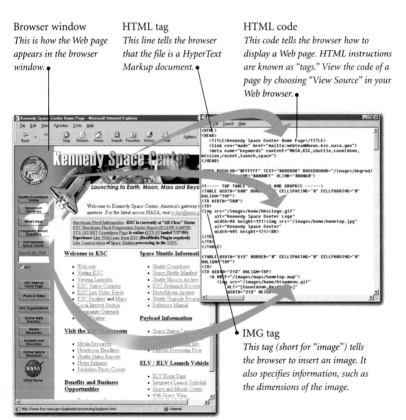

IMG tag
This tag (short for "image") tells the browser to insert an image. It also specifies information, such as the dimensions of the image.

SEARCHING WITH INTERNET EXPLORER

Searching the Web for information is undoubtedly one of the most common things you will do online. Unless you look for a known Web address , you will use a collection of programs and free services commonly known as "search engines."

1 CLICK SEARCH
• Click the **Search** button on the Toolbar. A frame will appear in the left of your browser window.

2 SEARCH CATEGORY
• Type a search term in the search text box and click on **Search**.
• Note that there is a **Customize** button in this frame. Clicking on this allows you to choose the categories of search available and which search engines you wish to use.

3 LIST OF HITS
• When the list of hits appears in the left-hand frame, hold the mouse pointer over any entry to see the address and a brief description of the Website. Click any entry to display that site in the main part of the browser window.

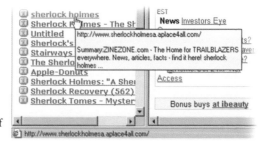

38 Using a Web address

37 What is a search engine?

WHAT IS A SEARCH ENGINE?

There are two types of search engine: the *search index* is a vast catalog made up of every word taken from all the Web pages searched by a program called a "bot" or spider, which crawls through the Web and returns its information to the index; the *Web directory* is compiled by real people who organize Web pages into categories and subcategories, allowing you to search very effectively. The most popular search engines now combine both principles. Your Web browser will connect to search engines to seek information, but you can also go directly to a search engine's Website (using its Web address ⬜) to take advantage of more advanced features. The screen below is from the Yahoo! Website.

Enter a search term here and click on the **Search** *button.*

The advanced search option is recommended for greater relevance in your results.

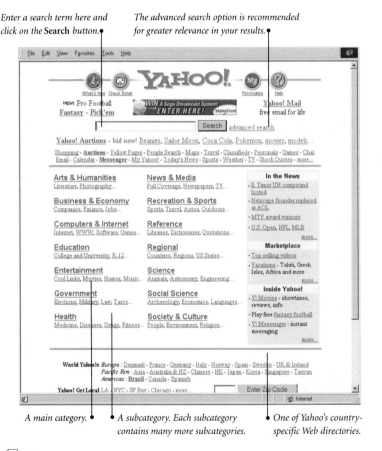

A main category.

A subcategory. Each subcategory contains many more subcategories.

One of Yahoo's country-specific Web directories.

USING A WEB ADDRESS

Website addresses are now a common sight in magazines, on products, and at the end of television and radio programs. If you know the address of the Website that you want to visit, your Web browser will take you straight to it if you simply type this address in the address bar at the top of the screen.

1 CLEARING THE ADDRESS BAR

● Before you can type in a new address, you must first clear the current contents. Position the cursor anywhere in the address field and click once.

● The contents of the address bar are highlighted.

● Press the ← Bksp key to delete the contents.

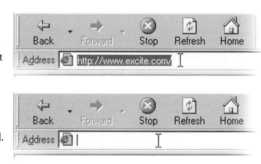

2 TYPING THE ADDRESS

● Now type the full address, taking care to copy exactly all the spelling and punctuation.

3 CONNECTING TO THE SITE

● Once you have typed the address, click on the **Go** button to the right of the address or press the Enter↵ key. Once the connection is made, the Web page will start to appear on your screen.

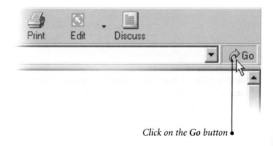

Click on the Go button ●

ADDING FAVORITES

If you intend to visit a Web page frequently, make it one of your "Favorites." Favorites are essentially shortcuts to Web pages or Websites and are stored in your Favorites folder. You access them from the drop-down list that appears when you click the **Favorites** menu. The contents of the Favorites folder, like any other in Windows 98, can be organized in any way you choose ⌐.

1 CHOOSING A FAVORITE

● When a page is in your browser window that you wish to add to your Favorites list, first choose **Add to Favorites** from the **Favorites** menu.

A folder of Favorites ●

BEING METHODICAL

If you want to be more methodical about adding a Favorite, you can make certain adjustments when you first save it. For example, when the **Add Favorite** box appears ⌐, you can overtype the entry that automatically appears in the **Name** box. (Sometimes this automatic entry for the **Name** box is not particularly memorable, so it is worth typing something that identifies the site more usefully for you.) You can then choose an existing folder in which to save the Favorite, or you can create a new folder and drop your Favorite straight into it.

This is precisely what you do when you choose to use the **Organize Favorites** feature.

41 Organizing Your Favorites

40 Adding a favorite

2 ADDING A FAVORITE

● Click **OK** in the **Add Favorite** dialog box that appears.

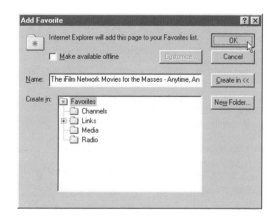

3 RETURNING TO A FAVORITE

● The Favorite you have just added will appear at the bottom of your Favorites list. To return to this page, just select it from the **Favorites** list.

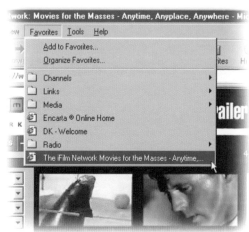

SAVING IMAGES AS WALLPAPER

Internet Explorer can set a Web image as your Windows wallpaper. Right-click the image itself, and then choose **Set As Wallpaper** from the pop-up menu that appears onscreen.

ORGANIZING YOUR FAVORITES

It makes sense to keep your Favorites organized in labeled folders. This will save you time and make it much easier to browse through your favorite Web pages.

Edit your Favorites list while you are off-line and be sure to choose clear labels for your folders so that you won't be left wondering what is stored where.

1 ORGANIZE FAVORITES
● Click **Organize Favorites** on the **Favorites** menu.

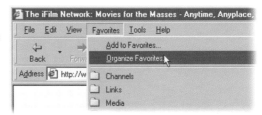

2 MAKE CHANGES
● In the **Organize Favorites** box you can rename any Favorite, move it into an existing folder, or create new folders. Any changes you make here will appear the next time you access your Favorites list.

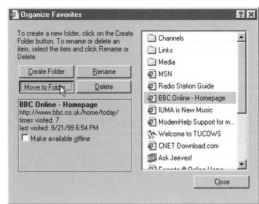

Favorites as HTML
You can export all your favorites into HTML format if you prefer ⬜. Then all these shortcuts automatically become hotlinks on your own private Web page.

35 **How a Web Page Works**

VIEWING THE FAVORITES LIST

You can access the Favorites list by clicking the **Favorites** menu. Holding the cursor over any folder icon will activate a submenu. If you prefer to see your Favorites onscreen while you browse, click the **Favorites** button on the toolbar. A frame will appear in the left of the browser window containing your Favorites list. To close, click the X in the top right-hand corner.

DETAILS OF YOUR FAVORITES

When viewing Favorites in the left frame of the browser window, note that the title and the Universal Resource Locator (URL) of the link appears when you hold the mouse pointer over its name in the list. In some cases, additional information about the Web page also appears.

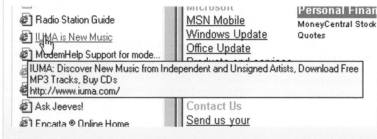

Change Your Home page

If you would like your browser always to open with your favorite page, do the following: Make sure the relevant page is in the browser window. Choose **Internet Options** from the Tools menu. The **Internet** **Options** dialog box will then appear. Under the General tab, click on the **Use Current** under the **Home page** section.

BROWSING THE WEB OFFLINE

Offline browsing is a very useful feature that enables you to store Web pages or even an entire Website on your hard drive. This is especially useful if you wish to spend time browsing a site without tying up the telephone line or running up unnecessary connection charges (if you have to pay them).It can also be of use if you wish to read certain Websites on a portable computer while traveling, since an Internet connection is obviously not required while browsing offline. You can specify Websites for offline browsing when you use the **Add to Favorites** feature.

To browse offline, choose **Work Offline** from the **File** menu.

1 CHOOSING THE PAGE

● From the Web page you wish to save for offline browsing, choose **Add to Favorites** from the **Favorites** menu.

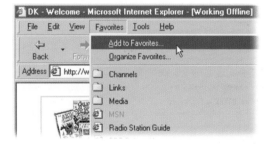

2 MAKING THE PAGE AVAILABLE

● In the **Add Favorite** dialog box, tick the check box next to **Make available offline**.
● Then click **Customize…**

Checkbox for offline browsing options

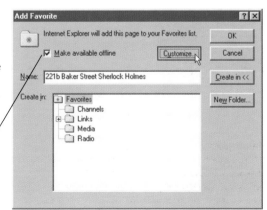

3 USING THE WIZARD

● Now follow the instructions in the **Offline Favorite Wizard**.

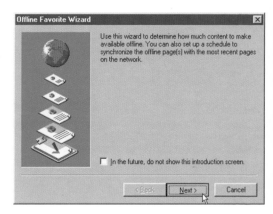

Advanced Options

You can nominate any Favorite for offline browsing by right-clicking it in the Favorites list. If you have already nominated a Favorite for offline browsing, you can start the synchronization process by right-clicking it and choosing **Synchronize** from the drop-down menu.

WHAT CAN I ACCESS OFFLINE?

Next time you are working offline, start your browser and look at your Favorites list. You can view any pages offline that appear in bold type. Entries that are grayed out will be unavailable offline. The shape of the mouse pointer will indicate whether or not a page is available.

4 UNAVAILABLE WEB PAGES

● If you click a link that is unavailable offline, the **Web page unavailable while offline** dialog box will appear, giving the option to connect to your ISP.

DO A LITTLE RESEARCH

The **Offline Favorite Wizard** asks you how many "links deep" you wish to download from the page you have chosen for offline browsing. It is worth exploring the site a little before deciding what is a sensible setting for this box. If you choose to save links two levels deep without checking things out first, you may inadvertently save some very large, unwanted files to your hard drive.

SYNCHRONIZING PAGES

To keep the Web pages that you have stored on your computer up to date, your browser will need to visit the appropriate sites to update the pages while you are online. This process is known as synchronizing the pages.

WHEN TO SYNCHRONIZE

You can specify how often this is done, and at what time of day. Unless you need to synchronize a large number of offline pages, your browser can perform this task in the background while you are browsing the Web. To manage these tasks, choose **Synchronize** from the Tools menu and type the relevant settings in the **Items to Synchronize** dialog box.

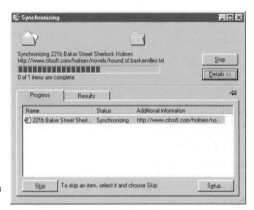

The synchronization process is shown above.

MULTIMEDIA ON THE WEB

Over the last five years, Web pages have come alive with animations, sounds, a host of multimedia effects, and ever more ingenious interactive elements.

The introduction of new technologies such as Java and ActiveX, applications like RealPlayer and Shockwave, and significant enhancements to HTML (the "tagged" language in which Web pages are written), have brought exciting new multimedia capabilities and levels of interactivity to the Web.

LIVE ON THE WEB

Multimedia applications still do not run as smoothly as they would from a CD or DVD-ROM (unless you have a state-of-the-art Internet connection), but the performance of Web-based multimedia improves almost monthly; unlike the CD-ROM, the Web can deliver "live" TV and radio broadcasts.

USING INTERNET EXPLORER

Internet Explorer is capable of handling most of the multimedia file types that appear on Web pages, but some pages contain files that will not "run" without additional software called a "plug-in." You can download new plug-ins or upgrade existing ones from the developers' sites, from specialized software sites, or from the CDs that come with computer magazines. You will know if a Web page requires a particular plug-in because it will tell you so.

There are many television and radio stations to be found on the Web.

DOWNLOADING THE NECESSARY SOFTWARE

If your browser meets a file type that it doesn't know how to handle, you will be given the option to download the relevant software, or 'plug-in,' to enable you to continue viewing that page. If you agree to download the software, you are usually taken to the home page for the maker of that plug-in to find out more about it before deciding whether you want to proceed ⌐.

RADIO

As well as Internet-only radio stations, many national and local stations broadcast live over the Internet. These will run in the background while you browse the Web. Internet Explorer's Radio Guide provides links to many radio stations.

THE RADIO TOOLBAR

● To access the radio Toolbar, choose **Toolbars** from the **View** menu and then **Radio** from the drop-down menu.

● From the **Radio** toolbar, choose **Radio Station Guide** from the **Radio Stations** drop-down menu. Many links to radio stations are provided on this page, arranged by country, region, or category.

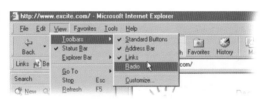

ONLINE GAMING

The Internet has a lot to offer the computer games enthusiast. For a start, producers of commercial games software have their own sites, which contain, for example, news, upgrades, competitions, and special offers. But these are far outnumbered by the sites offering hints, cheats, and links to virtually every computer game ever produced. These pages are created by the games' players – with an enthusiasm and devotion sometimes verging on the fanatical!

MULTIPLAYER
Many games today have multiplayer online capabilities. If you have a working modem plugged in and ready to go, you can use a menu within such games to gain access automatically to servers on the Internet on which the game is being played. For an excellent list of online games visit ☐:
http://directory.hotbot. com/games/.

SOLO GAMES, PUZZLES, AND TRIVIA
The crossword puzzle on this site is changed daily. Click on any of the squares to highlight the appropriate across or down entry; then type the solution. If you want to change your entry, you can simply overtype it.

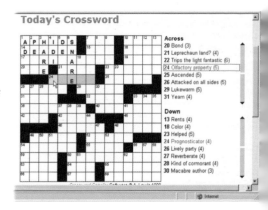

GAMES ROOMS

If you prefer playing against a real opponent, join one of the many games rooms on the Internet.

The MSN Gaming Zone offers a selection of games. Go to zone.msn.com and click **Game Index** in the left-hand margin.

Below is an example of a backgammon game.

Chat with your opponent by typing in this box. •

Drag and drop the counters to move them. •

Click on the dice to "roll" them when it is your turn. •

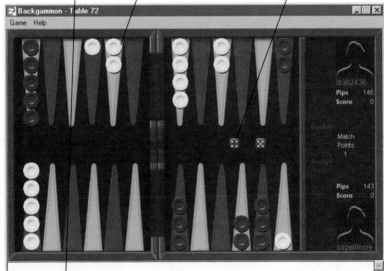

DOWNLOADING FROM THE INTERNET

The Internet is full of free stuff – books, help files, sound and video clips, photographs, screen-savers, software, lists of links to free stuff, and so on. In fact, you can download the images from any Web page you visit simply by right-clicking the image and choosing **Save Picture as…** from the drop-down menu.

WHAT IS FREEWARE?

Copyright exists as much on the Internet as anywhere else. But there are thousands of things that are absolutely free for you to download, keep, and use.

Downloading software from the Web is easy. You will usually click a download button on the Web page, or a link that begins the process for you. The installer file in this example was found on www.download.com.

Freeware only
The instructions on these pages relate only to the downloading of "free" software.

1 CLICKING TO DOWNLOAD
● The item that you are wishing to download should have a **Download** button. Click on this.

RealJukebox Basic *new **popular** pick*

- Download Now
- Developer's Site
- All Downloa
- Product Spe

2 SAVING THE PROGRAM
● When the **File Download** dialog box appears, ensure the **Save this program to disk** option is checked and click **OK**.

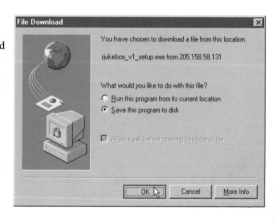

3 CHOOSING A LOCATION

● In the **Save As** dialog box, choose a location to save the file. (In this example, the file will be saved in a folder called **downloads**.) Then click on **Save**.

4 MONITORING AND INSTALLING

● A window will then appear showing the progress of the downloading.

● When the file has finished downloading, you will need to open the folder in which you saved it and double-click the file. The software's installation program should then take care of the rest of the installation.

● It is best to carry out the installation after you have finished your online session, because installation may require you to restart your computer, thereby ending your online session. Some programs run the installation process automatically, simply prompting you for information or a click on a proceed button. This is often the case for self-installing browser plug-ins.

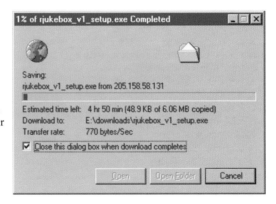

SHAREWARE AND FREEWARE

Shareware is software that is free to try for a limited period. When the time is up you should pay up or stop using it! It is increasingly common for shareware to time itself out at the end of the trial period. Freeware is software that you can keep and use, but is still protected by copyright.

Public domain software is free, and may be altered and used for profit. But the author has to state explicitly that it is public domain. Registering any software can bring many benefits – free upgrades, documentation, extra features, and the know-ledge that you are funding further software.

EMAIL

For many people, electronic mail is one of the most important reasons for getting connected to the Internet. It enables you to send messages to anyone, anywhere, who has an email address.

USING EMAIL

With an email software program, you can write letters on your PC, address them to the destination email address, and send them winging their way around the globe in a matter of moments. You can also enclose images and even video clips.

SIGNING UP
When you sign up for a new Internet account, you will receive one or more unique email addresses. Outlook Express, which is supplied as part of Windows 98, contains an email client program that enables you both to send and receive email.

Speed is relative
Although email can be lightning fast, your mail might as well be delivered by mule if the recipient doesn't check the mail! Email can only be delivered when the recipient requests new mail from the server.

ADVANTAGES AND DISADVANTAGES OF EMAIL

ADVANTAGES OF EMAIL
There are many advantages to using email rather than conventional mail. First, it is cheap – never usually costing more than the price of a local phone call to send. Secondly, it is very fast. If all connections are working effectively, an email message can be received by the addressee within minutes of your sending the message, regardless of location. You can also "attach" files to your email messages (for example, documents, spreadsheets, photographs, and sound clips).

DISADVANTAGES OF EMAIL
Email is less private than conventional mail since its contents could be read by anyone with access to your, or the recipient's, computer. It is therefore wise not to send anything too sensitive via email unless you have some way of protecting the contents – by using encryption software, for instance. For more information on secure email, refer to **Sending secure messages** in the Outlook Express **Help** file).

GET THE ADDRESS RIGHT

It is especially important with electronic mail that you get the address absolutely right. Unlike conventional mail, there isn't a local mailman who can use some judgment if an address is nearly right.

Email is entirely mechanical, so "nearly right" is simply wrong. Any wrongly addressed mail will be automatically returned to sender (or "bounced back" as it is otherwise known) with a "failed to deliver" message from the remote server.

THE ELEMENTS THAT MAKE UP AN EMAIL ADDRESS

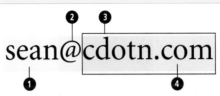

1 User Name
Identifies the addressee.
2 Separator
An @ ("at") symbol separates the user and domain names.
3 Domain name
Is the computer address, with periods separating the parts.

4 Suffix
The suffix "com" indicates a commercial organization based in the US. A company based in the UK would more commonly end with co.uk, although com and net are also frequently used. Other suffixes include gov for a

government organization, and edu or ac for an academic institution. All countries except the US also add an extra two-letter suffix. For the United Kingdom this is uk, il is for Israel, and nz is the New Zealand suffix.

HOW A MESSAGE IS SENT

When you have addressed and sent your message it is sent to your ISP's outgoing (SMTP) mail server. From here it is forwarded to the appropriate ISP. When it arrives at the ISP in the address, it is delivered to the recipient's "pigeon-hole." The next time the addressee checks his or her mail (by logging on to the ISP's POP3 server) the mail is delivered.

EMAIL ON THE MOVE

It is very useful to have more than one email account so that you can read messages on the move. Web-based email accounts are useful because you can log on to them via a secure Website from any computer with an Internet connection and retrieve and send mail. Microsoft offers a service called Hotmail

(you can sign up for an account from the opening screen of Outlook Express), and Yahoo offers a similar service (visit www.yahoo.com for information).

A word of warning, however. The more accounts you have, the longer it will take to trawl through them all to see if you have any messages.

WHAT OUTLOOK EXPRESS CAN DO

Outlook Express enables you to send and receive electronic mail messages, and to record and store all your email addresses and personal contact details, in the form of an electronic address book.

Outlook Express also enables you to create multiple users, so other people who wish to use your computer can receive their own email, and keep their contact details separately and privately from your own.

EMAIL

Outlook Express provides a user-friendly interface that makes it easy for you to compose, send, and receive your email messages working directly from the main window.

Email messages need not be just text; they can also contain pictures, hypertext links to Websites, and even self-contained file attachments. All of these will be sent at speed and for the price of a local call.

Customizing Outlook Express
If you like to personalize your software, Outlook Express has dozens of customizable features. You can access them all from the **Options** dialog box (choose **Options** from the **Tools** menu).

NEWSGROUPS

For those who have mastered the art of sending email and want to branch out into the world of online debate and discussion, Outlook Express provides a newsreading facility that enables you to read and join in with electronic "newsgroups" 🔲. Newsgroup discussions cover just about every topic under the sun, from world politics and all types of hobbies and leisure interests to more focused subjects, such as the life cycle of the dung beetle or sea turtle conservation.

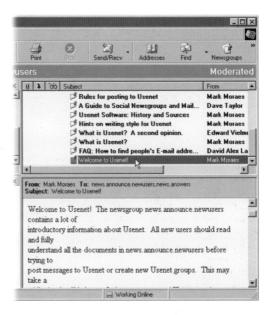

CONTACTS

You can use the Outlook Express address book to build an electronic database of personal and business contacts. For each contact you can record name, home, business, personal, and other details. You can then use these address book records to address emails without having to retype the address each time. The address book helps you to manage your email sessions more efficiently.

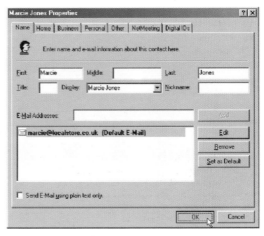

HOW TO SEND A MESSAGE

Creating email is extremely simple, as the following steps will show. All that you need is the email address of the recipient, and a dash of creativity for the message! From this point onward, everything is handled by the software.

1 STARTING A NEW MESSAGE

● Click the **New Mail** button. The **New Message** window will appear.

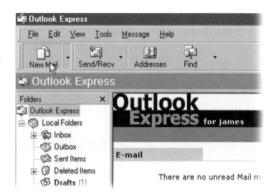

2 TYPING IN THE ADDRESS

● Type the email address of the addressee in the **To:** box.

If you want to copy the message to someone else, type his or her name in the **Cc:** box. Type a brief description of the message in the **Subject** line. (This is not compulsory, but helpful to the addressee, who may have many new messages to read through.)

3 TYPING IN YOUR MESSAGE

● Type your message in the main body of the message window. You can format your message using the standard text formatting toolbar, although for simple text messages this is not really necessary. When you have finished your message, click **Send**.

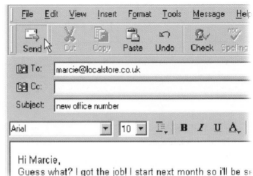

4 SENDING THE EMAIL

● Because you are working offline, a **Send Mail** information box will appear, informing you that the message has been placed in the Outbox until you next connect to your ISP and are running Outlook Express.

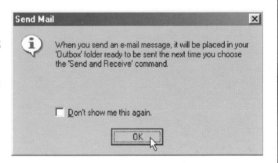

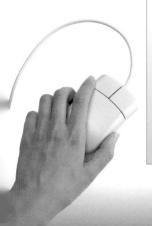

HOW OFTEN IS MY MAIL SENT OUT?

Every time you start up Outlook Express, any messages waiting in your **Outbox** are sent to your ISP, and any messages on your ISP's mail server that are addressed to you are delivered to your **Inbox**. While you remain online, this whole process will happen automatically every 30 minutes.

You can ask for mail to be sent and delivered immediately by clicking the **Send/Recv** button.

You can change these default settings by accessing the **Options** dialog box (choose **Options** from the Tools menu) and changing the settings under **Send/Receive messages**.

SETTING UP THE ADDRESS BOOK

Once you've added an address to the address book, you won't ever need to type it again when sending a message.

Adding a new entry to the address book in its simplest form is very easy to do and will take no more than a few seconds.

1 OPENING THE ADDRESS BOOK
● Click the **Addresses** button on the Outlook Express Toolbar.

2 CREATING A NEW CONTACT
● Click the **New** button and choose **New Contact...** from the drop-down menu.

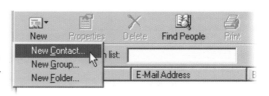

3 ADDING THE DETAILS
● In the **Properties** dialog box that appears, type the relevant name and email address. (The address book has many optional fields in which you can add home and business telephone numbers, addresses, and so on, but name and email address are the only fields required for email purposes.) When you have finished, click **OK**.

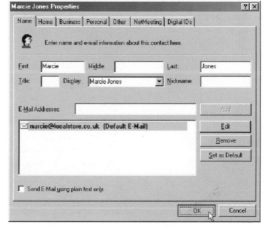

4 THE LIST OF CONTACTS

● The new entry to your address book will now appear as a name in the **Contacts** panel of the main Outlook Express window.

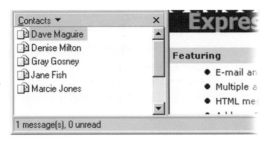

USING THE ADDRESS BOOK

The next time you want to send a message to someone who is already listed in your address book, open the **New Message** window and click the **To:** icon (to the left of the **To:** box). Your address book will automatically appear.

1 SELECTING ADDRESSEES

● Choose a name from the list and click **To:>**. (You can select multiple addressees by holding down the Ctrl key while you click on the appropriate names.)

Click on names

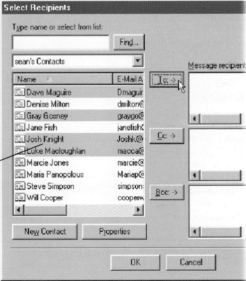

2 ENTERING ADDRESSEES

● The names will appear in the **To:** box in the **New Message** window, and you can proceed as normal.

ORGANIZING YOUR EMAIL

Without organization, it won't be long before the contents of your **Inbox** becomes unmanageable. If you subscribe to any of the thousands of daily mailing lists ⌐ available on the Internet, you will soon have a huge list of mail received. Fortunately, it is very easy to organize email in Outlook Express.

1 CREATING A FOLDER

● Click **Local folders** in the Folders panel, choose **New** from the **File** menu, and then **Folder...** from the drop-down menu.

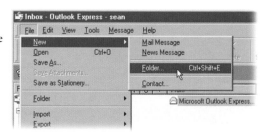

2 NAMING THE FOLDER

● In the **Create Folder** dialog box, type a name for the new folder in the **Folder name** box, and click on **OK**.

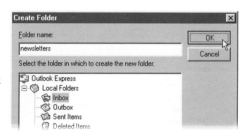

61 Mailing Lists and Newsletters

3 VIEWING THE SAVED FOLDER

- In this example, a folder called **newsletters** is created in the **Inbox** folder.
- You can drag and drop messages at any time from the main message list (on the right) to any of the folders in the folders panel (on the left).

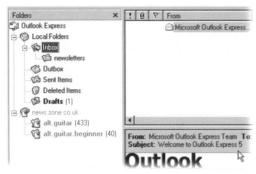

MAILING LISTS AND NEWSLETTERS

Internet mailing lists can prove to be a useful way of receiving information without actually needing to look for it. Thousands of newsletters exist, catering to all sorts of interests. You can subscribe to many of these newsletters by supplying your email address in the appropriate box on the Web page.

UNSUBSCRIBING

Unsubscribing is usually equally painless. Every newsletter should supply you with details on how to remove your name from their list when you decide that the information that they provide is no longer of use to you.

www.liszt.com •
Visit this Website for a directory of 90,000 mailing lists, plus useful background and subscription information for most of these lists.

NEWSGROUPS

Newsgroups on the Internet are rarely concerned with "news" in the sense of current affairs. They are essentially public email discussion forums devoted to a wide range of topics and interests.

USING NEWSGROUPS

Newsgroups provide a forum for people to discuss topics of mutual interest and share information – whether highly technical or just gossip. They can be excellent places to get advice if, for example, you have a computer problem. Participants (or "subscribers," to use the correct term) "post" messages to be seen and be responded to, either publicly or privately, by any reader of that newsgroup.

A WEALTH OF INFORMATION

When you connect to a particular news server and download the full list of available newsgroups, you can scroll through the list and choose to view any that interest you.

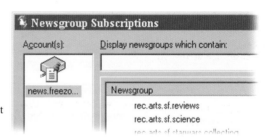

WHAT IS USENET?

Usenet is the name given to the large body of newsgroups (there are currently more than 30,000 of them) distributed around the world by computers known as news servers. These servers exchange information so that each one carries a copy of the most recent messages. Usenet is not, strictly speaking, part of the Internet, although Internet sites are used to carry its newsgroups.

Most ISPs provide access to Usenet newsgroups, usually via their own news servers.

SETTING UP OUTLOOK EXPRESS AS A NEWSREADER

If Outlook Express has not been set up as a newsreader you will need to do this in order to access the newsgroups.

Remember that you need to be online to download the newsgroups, and this may take ten minutes or so.

1 ACCESSING THE DEFAULT PAGE

● Access the default Outlook Express page by clicking **Outlook Express** at the top of the **Folders** panel.

2 SETTING UP AN ACCOUNT

● Under the heading **Newsgroups** click on **Set up a Newsgroups account....**

3 ENTERING NEWS SERVER NAME

● The Internet Connection Wizard will now appear. The easy set-up procedure is very similar to that described for setting up an email account 🗋, but here you need to type the name of your news server as provided by your ISP.

● You will now be given the option to download all available newsgroups.

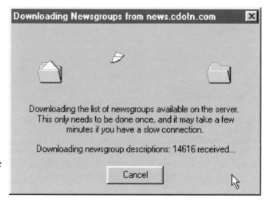

Downloading Newsgroups from news.cdotn.com

Downloading the list of newsgroups available on the server. This only needs to be done once, and it may take a few minutes if you have a slow connection.

Downloading newsgroup descriptions: 14616 received...

Cancel

27 Setting up an Email Account

READING MESSAGES IN A NEWSGROUP

The **Newsgroup Subscriptions** window shows the name of the news server in the left panel and the names of newsgroups available to you in the main panel on the right. You are now ready to read messages from your chosen newsgroup.

1 NEWSGROUPS SUBSCRIPTIONS

● To view the **Newsgroup Subscriptions** window, choose **Newsgroups** from the Tools menu.

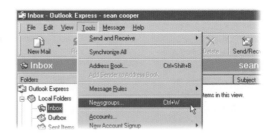

2 LOCATING A NEWSGROUP

● To locate a chosen newsgroup, type a key word in the **Display newsgroups which contain:** box.

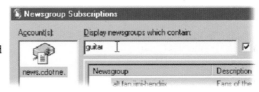

3 VIEWING A GROUP

● To view the contents of a group, click the name in the list and click the **Subscribe** button.

4 DOWNLOADING A MESSAGE

● To download a message, simply double-click on it.

Subject	From
Re: gibson SG	MM
Re: REQ: Driving directions to the actu...	HJ
Re: CLASSIC ROCK-n-ROLL QUOTES	mb@c
Re: Slowest guitar player	NF

POSTING TO A NEWSGROUP

The procedure for posting a message to a newsgroup is basically the same as sending an email to a friend. The only real difference is that your words will be published for all the newsgroup's subscribers to read.

1 HIGHLIGHTING A MESSAGE

● Highlight the message to which you wish to reply. Click the **Reply Group** button.

2 ENTERING YOUR REPLY

● Type your reply into the email reply window that appears, and click **Send**.

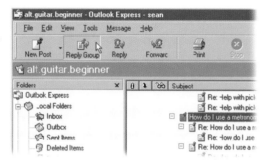

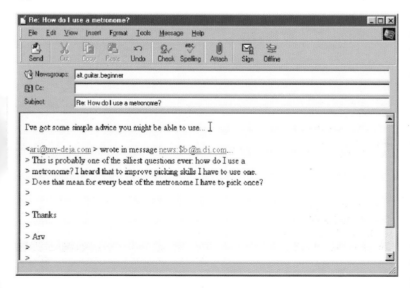

CHATTING LIVE

"Internet chat" refers to online real-time conversations via the keyboard. Anything that you type will appear almost instantly on the monitors of people who are logged-in to that chat room.

CHAT ROOMS

To chat with other Internet users, you need a chat "client" program and an Internet chat "room" to use it in. These are available on a number of Websites and will allow you to have "conversations" with all manner of people from all over the world. You will have the option of speaking to everyone in the room or, should you prefer, talking one-to-one with another visitor to the chat room.

WHAT TO DISCUSS?

Chat is currently big on the Web, with many Websites offering moderated chat areas where you can meet other users to gossip, flirt, argue, chat, and maybe even discuss whatever the site was set up to discuss! Some sites – especially those belonging to broadcasting and media companies – may provide "celebrity" chat sessions giving visitors the opportunity to put questions to authors, rock stars, politicians, and so on. These are regular features of the online services, available to subscribers.

By entering our rooms, you agree to abide by our CHAT R

Handle	sean
Email Address:	*(optic*
Chat Room:	The Net Cafe
Line Count:	30

No Frames — Enter Chat Room

Entering the chat room
This image shows someone logging in to a chat site.
The user's "handle" need not be his or her real name.

CHAT SET-UP

Chat is becoming increasingly easy to set up and use on the Web. Some sites require you to download and install a plug-in to participate. You may also be asked to fill in a registration form. Others require no configuration or plug-ins – you simply go to the Web page and join in.

Connecting to a chat room is easy. All you need to do is choose a user name, type in your email address, and wait briefly before entering the lobby.

In the early days of the Net, Internet Relay Chat (IRC) was the most widely used chat medium. It is still very popular, but seems bewilderingly fast to a beginner.

The screen shown on this page is typical of most chat client programs, allowing you to read the conversation and compose your reply on the same screen.

The main panel shows the ongoing "public" conversation. All users of the room are listed in this panel. Double-click any user's name to speak privately to him or her (you can never really be sure).

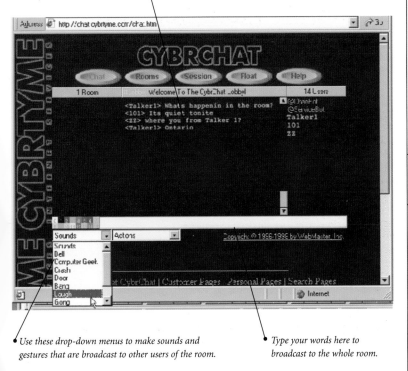

Use these drop-down menus to make sounds and gestures that are broadcast to other users of the room.

Type your words here to broadcast to the whole room.

47 Downloading the necessary software

CHATTING IN 3D WORLDS

Online 3D chat environments fall somewhere between online games, chat areas, and virtual communities.

In some of these multi-user environments you can actually build your own virtual dwelling, trade, and take part in competitions as well as chatting with the other online "residents." The example shown here – Microsoft's V-Chat – offers a typical 3D chat environment. When you first run V-Chat you are

asked to choose a user name and an avatar to represent you. An avatar is the 3D figure that will represent you. You can use

it to move around the chat zones and to display a range of gestures and facial expressions to the group to which you are talking.

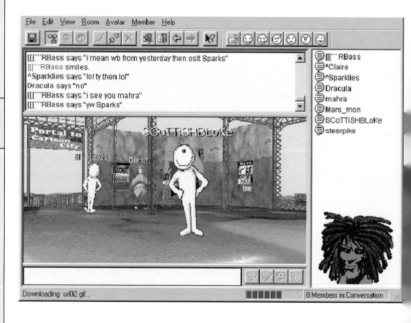

EMOTICONS AND ABBREVIATIONS

As your experience of sending and receiving email grows, you may notice strange punctuation symbols in some messages that you read. These are called "emoticons" (emotional icons) and they are used in email and other electronic communications to convey humor and emotion in a typed medium where it can be easy to misinterpret the intention and tone of what is being said. Emoticons resemble facial expressions when viewed with your head tilted to the left. Here are some of the more common emoticons and abbreviations and what they mean.

: -)	Happy	AFAIK	As far as I know
: -))	Very happy	BRB	Be right back
: - (	Sad	BTW	By the way
: - ((	Very sad	CUL or CUL8R	See you later
: - /	Undecided	FAQ	Frequently asked question
: - p	Tongue-in-cheek		
: - *	Kissing	IMO	In my opinion
: - t	Angry	LOL	Laughing out loud
: - V	Shouting	OIC	Oh I see
: - O	Shocked	ROTFLOL	Rolling on the floor laughing out loud
: - {	Disapproving		
; -)	Winking	THK	Thanks

NETIQUETTE

When you communicate in the Internet's public spaces – newsgroups, chatrooms, online games, 3D virtual worlds, and so on – you need to observe certain codes of behavior. Much of this is common sense and everyday courtesy. Just remember that there is a real person at the other end of the line and you won't go far wrong. Here is some basic advice to follow:

• When you first enter a chat room, lurk for a while, read the messages, get a feel for the sort of discussions and the general style of conversation in the room. With newsgroups, it is very important that you read the frequently asked questions (FAQ) file for the group. If you ask a question that features prominently in the FAQ, you will not endear yourself to the regular users of the group.

• Don't SHOUT– typing in capital letters is known as shouting. It is universally disliked because blocks of text in capitals are hard to read.
• Be careful with humor – it can be difficult to convey humor or irony in a written form without giving offense – if you make a comment that you think might be ambiguous in tone, back it up with an emoticon.

GLOSSARY

CHAT
A conversation on the Internet between two or more people, in real time, via the keyboard.

DIAL-UP NETWORKING SOFTWARE
Windows 98 software that enables you to connect to the Internet via a service provider.

DOWNLOAD
The process of transferring a file from a remote computer to your computer.

EMAIL (ELECTRONIC MAIL)
A system for sending messages between computers that are linked electronically over a network.

FREEWARE
Software that can be freely used and distributed, but the author retains copyright.

HTML (HYPERTEXT MARK-UP LANGUAGE)
The "tagged" language in which Web pages are written.

HYPERLINKS
Part of a Web page (text, image, table etc.) that links to another document on the Internet.

HYPERTEXT
Text that contains links to other parts of a document, or to documents held on another computer. Clicking a hypertext link takes you directly to the linked document. Hypertext links on Web pages are usually highlighted or underlined.

INTERNET SERVICE PROVIDER (ISP)
A commercial organization that provides access to the Internet.

MODEM (MODULATOR-DEMODULATOR)
An electronic device that allows computers to communicate via a telephone line by converting signals between analog and binary forms.

NETIQUETTE
An unwritten code of conduct for the proper and polite usage of the Internet.

NETWORK
A group of interconnected computers that can exchange information.

NEWSREADER
Software that enables you to access and use newsgroups. Outlook Express has newsreader capabilities.

PLUG-IN
A program that adds features to a Web browser so that it can handle file types containing e.g. 3D and multimedia elements.

PROTOCOL
A set of rules that two computers must follow when they communicate. Software on networked computers must be designed to use these rules.

SEARCH ENGINE
Software that searches for information on the Internet based on your search criteria. Commonly applied to websites that host search facilities, such as www.yahoo.com.

SERVER
Any computer that allows users to connect to it and share information and resources held on it. The term also refers to the software that makes the information available for downloading.

SHAREWARE
Software that is made freely available for use on a try-before-you-buy basis.

TCP/IP (TRANSMISSION CONTROL PROTOCOL/ INTERNET PROTOCOL
The two core Internet protocols that define how data must be transferred between two computers.

URL (UNIVERSAL RESOURCE LOCATOR)
An address on the Internet. You type a URL into your browser to visit a website.

V-STANDARDS
Worldwide telecommunications standards that govern program-ming commands and data compression standards used by modems and other devices.

WEB BROWSER
A program used for viewing and accessing information on the Web. Microsoft Internet Explorer, and Netscape Navigator are the two most widely used Web browsers.

WORLD WIDE WEB (WWW, W3, THE WEB)
The collection of Websites on the Internet. These sites are connected using hyperlinks.

INDEX

ACKNOWLEDGMENTS

PUBLISHER'S ACKNOWLEDGMENTS
Dorling Kindersley would like to thank the following:
Paul Mattock of APM, Brighton, for commissioned photography.
Microsoft Corporation for permission to reproduce screens
from within Microsoft® FrontPage®, Microsoft® Internet Explorer,
and Microsoft® Outlook® Express.
bbc.co.uk; cnn.com; excite.com; freebeeb.net; gamesdomain.com; greenpeace.org;
ksc.nasa.gov; nfl.com; unicef.org; virgin.net; whitehouse.gov; yahoo!

PICTURE CREDITS
The Stock Market/Jeff Zaruba (p. 9).

Every effort has been made to trace the copyright holders.
The publisher apologizes for any unintentional omissions and would be pleased,
in such cases, to place an acknowledgment in future editions of this book.